Into the Psych Ward
by Kendrick Sims

A True Story

November 2nd – 10th, 2023

COPYRIGHT 2025 KENDRICK SIMS
FIRST PUBLISHED 2025
PRINTED IN THE UNITED STATES OF AMERICA

Books by Kendrick Ashton Sims

2018
The Bully
Lazar & Jingles with Bunson in Holiday Gifts
Lazar & Jingles with Bunson in Mirrors in Strange Place

2019
Lazar & Jingles with Bunson in Stars Cease to Shine
Mr. Wolfy Goes to the Vet
Cooper Corner
Ariel

2020
A Sleepy Tail
A Kitties Dream
Chip
Lazar & Jingles with Bunson in
Backpacks and Blue Roses
Chip and Friends

2021
A Silence in the Stars
Lazar & Jingles with Bunson
in Showers of Sorrow

2022
Cubby
Lazar & Jingles with Bunson
in Animals Go to Heaven

2023
Lazar & Jingles present:
The Fallen Snow - A Suicide in Waterford
Alice
Lazar & Jingles with Bunson present:
Found Among You
Waterford's Requiem
Poems and Pictures by Kendrick Sims

2024
Salem
Fears Lonely Path
Flap Your Arms
Farts Aren't Beneath Me
The Clouds Weep Christmas Feelings

2025
Mr. Chip and Family
Into the Psych Ward: A True Story

To the woman I refer to as "Gail."
I could never have endured so much in such a short
period of time without you at my side.
I will always consider you my friend.

Kendrick Sims
February 2025.

The names of patients and hospital staff have been changed
in order to protect their privacy.

Into the Psych Ward
A True Story

Prologue.
Thursday, November 2nd, 2023.

As I made an effort to arise out of my bed there was a complete and total collapse. It was not entirely unexpected, it was simply unfortunate. I could not find the willpower, strength, nor the motivation to walk. I'd been up all night long. Not only that, I'd been wide awake for several nights during the month of October 2023. During those weeks of restlessness little peace had come to me. In the early morning hours of November 2nd, 2023 I'd reached the end of human endurance and I could no longer function. I was no longer able to take care of myself. I could not do the most basic of things. Brushing my teeth, combing my hair, shaving, taking a shower or even just walk down the stairs. These things were now impossible for me. All I could do is what I did, and that would be to call for help. I dialed 911. This was not the first time I'd called for the EMT's to come rescue me, but it was the most serious.

During the several months leading up to this morning crash my health had been in steep decline. From August 2023 up until that fateful morning just mentioned, I suffered a severe upper respiratory infection, gastrointestinal problems, urinary tract infections, as well as an increasing mental decline that was somehow related to my physical weaknesses. My interests became less, my daily capabilities shrank to near non-existence, and my down time increased drastically. Many medications were prescribed for both body and mind. Some helped, some didn't and some made me worse. Over those long late-Summer months those illnesses eventually began to subside, but the stress of constant illness and the lethargy it left me with took a huge toll on my mental health. It also left me incapable of caring for my dearest of friends. My cats.

During this period my furrever friends started becoming sick too. My furrever friends, I lost three of my beloved fur babies in a short amount of time. Two were twenty years old and another, Arnold, I did not know his age, but he was elderly. Tinker and Missy died from kidney failure. Arnold died from cancer. About a year prior I lost my fourteen year old Wolfy to gastro-intestinal issues. Losing these four friends so dear to me along with my bad health sent me into spiraling depression. One of which I didn't even know I was suffering at the time. I thought I was in mourning. That was true but there was much more going on in my head than I was admitting to. Denial is one of the stages of grief, and it's easy to get stuck in that state. The sadness, the illness, the loss, the strain, all of it combined was too much for me. I could not handle the strain of the past combined with the daily stresses of life. The toll of grief and agony accumulated on the night of November 2nd, 2023.

Nothing comes without a catalyst. The proverbial straw that breaks the camels back. November 1st, 2023 had been nothing short of abysmal. For weeks I'd been suffering from a long term anal tear, only I did not know it at the time. All I knew was that I was in pain and an anal tear is as painful as it sounds. It is continual pain all day and all night. Such things do not rest. Without treatment it does not heal. It simply persists. November 1st was my appointment with a gastroenterologist. It was an appointment that I'd had to wait several weeks for, and for the entirety of the waiting period I suffered from the pain of the tear. I suffered when I was walking, laying down, standing still or trying to sleep. I thought perhaps I had a hemorrhoid that wasn't healing. I honestly did not know. All I knew is that I could not wait for the appointment day to arrive. The doctor would make everything better. She just had to. I was in complete misery.

November 1st came and I found myself in the office of my gastroenterologist. After her examination I learned that it was not a hemorrhoid that I suffered, but an anal tear, and it would take weeks to heal, if not longer. There was nothing that could be done for it other than apply a specially formulated cream to the wound and wait for the body to heal itself. After being in pain for several weeks this was not the news I wanted to hear. Things were made even worse when the compounding pharmacy said it could take two weeks for them to formulate the cream. That was the news that sent me into all out panic. Not a panic attack per-se, but unending fear, stress and anxiety caused by the thought of two more weeks in agony. Fortunately for me the compounding pharmacy got the cream to me that very day, but the damage had already been done. Months of illness and sorrow combined with weeks of constant pain and a day of lost hope sent me into a full fledged panic attack that repeated itself at will. The totality of the night has been lost to me. Most of my memories regarding the night of November 1st lay buried under a deep layer of solid rock. However, I do remember talking to someone on the suicide and crisis hotline, or 988. It was a number I had called before. It was one among many crisis hotlines. The woman I spoke with was supportive, kind and understanding. However, she could not help me beyond the suggestion that I'd already taken time and time again. Go to the emergency room. I was leery of this course of action because I was afraid of emergency medical technicians. They'd proven to be unreliable, untrustworthy and callous. Several times I'd made a call for help. With the arrival of the ambulance I was told I did not need any assistance. They'd take me to the hospital if I wanted, but I'd be better off at home. EMT's should not be allowed to give medical advice. All they did was prolong my suffering and made me feel crazy. The woman I was talking to on 988 did convince me that I was in desperate need of help beyond what I'd been getting from my family doctor, as well as those in the emergency room. She told me that I needed to call 911 and go back to the ER and demand treatment. After speaking with her for nearly an hour I felt better, but I was not convinced. It was not until I tried to lay myself down to sleep that I knew she was right. The panic attack that this woman had talked me through over a period of forty-five minutes returned, and in full force. It did not and would not leave. I could not sleep. I could not eat. I could barely walk to the bathroom. All I could do is lay in bed, exhausted and afraid.

Enter into the early morning hours of November 2nd, 2023, and after a sleepless night I tried to get up to feed my cats. I could not do it. My legs would not work properly and I had to cling to the walls to maintain a standing position. I was physically, emotionally and mentally spent. I knew I was going to call 911, go to the emergency room and be admitted into the hospital. However, prior to that action only one thing mattered to me. I simply had to give my cat Alice her special cat food. I somehow managed that small task, because she had to be fed often and fed a certain type of food. After getting Alice her breakfast I collapsed onto my upstairs hallway floor and called 911.

The immediate aftermath of the phone call is not clear to me. The next thing I remember is having been taken from my upstairs hallway down into my living room, where they were prepping me to get into the ambulance. What happened next remained a mystery for a time, however after many more months of therapy I now know what occurred. My conscious mind retreated into itself and cocooned, only nobody knew this at the time. While events were transpiring I was labeled as a catatonic. That was how I arrived to the hospital at around 6:00 am. Catatonic, non-responsive and disassociated from reality. I recall the doctors trying to speak to me, but my consciousness was closed off and I could not form words to respond to them. It was as if I were watching a movie and everyone around me was nothing more or less than actors and actresses performing parts. They had no reality nor importance to their existence. All I could do was watch and listen to their actions around me. I could not interact in any way whatsoever.

Minutes passed quite slowly and my next recollection was coming out of my shell. I was able to get my phone out and made a phone call. How I happened to have my phone is a story as sad as it is short. This was my seventh time being taken to the emergency room within thirty days. The EMT's knew me and my plight all too well. They would just make sure my phone and identification were under me on my new bed as they left me in the hospital. All I had to do was reach under me and grab my phone. It's not such an easy endeavor when I'm still regaining my ability to move and talk, however I pressed the speaker button and I called the only person who could help. My mother.

I do not recall what was said during this conversation, or if much of anything were said at all. My memories of my time in the emergency room are dim, and with cause. It was a time of great misery. The lights were off, the ward was full and the nurses were doing nothing but sitting around the nurses station, babbling about whatever was going on in their lives. Not in the ER mind you, but in their lives. This was something that would not change during the entire eighteen hours I would be in that house of horrors. The nurses were of no help to me or to anyone who had come there looking for help. Yet one bright spot remained, my mom knew I was there and she was on her way. As I awaited her arrival the doctors began circling their latest arrival.

The doctors on duty were fine and considerate for the most part. Unlike the nurse counterparts in that they were knowledgeable if overworked. However, they were not psychiatrists. They could not help me. This had been proven by my previous stays in this very same ER. The doctor's were out of their league. I needed a psychiatrist and so I received three, all of which arrived shortly. I was not able to answer their questions beyond simple one or two word responses. Maybe a sentence here or there was given, but not often. It was immediately clear that I was unable to look after myself and needed mental help. With my consent and with their approval I was admitted to the hospital and officially became a psychiatric patient. If things had gone differently, this is where the story of my entrance into the psych ward would come to a satisfactory conclusion. However, things did not go well. Doctors have to do physical examinations, blood work, x-rays and the like before someone can be admitted into the psych ward. I would quickly receive all such tests and was deemed healthy for transfer, except for one irregular test result. Alone due to ignorance, this one irregularity caused me to remain stationary in the emergency room for eighteen straight hours.

My lab work did not indicate a life or death situation. My x-rays were fine. My pulse and blood pressure were normal. What was found were that my electrolytes were unusual, or so it was believed at the time. Because of this I could not be sent straight up to the psych ward, but had to be held until a bed could be found in the regular part of the hospital where patients are treated for physical problems. The problem was that there were no beds available in the entire hospital, and so I had to remain in the emergency room, stationary, unmoving and still suffering completely uncontrolled panic attacks.

There's not much to be said for any stay in the ER. However, when a person is having a mental meltdown and is suffering chronic panic attacks, being left alone in such a place is a hell that is impossible to describe. For this hell exists not only within ones own mind but around oneself as well. Everything and everyone is seen as a threat. There is no discerning between doctor or patient, kindness or cruelty. Add this, the state of the emergency room certainly did not help my feelings of security, as there were human beings screaming out for help all around me, others laying seemingly lifeless and unmoving. Outside of my cocooned state I could hear long, drawn-out arguments between patients who did not want to be there and their doctor. Then, of course, were the nurses, who did not seem to want to be there either. They would not make sure their patients were fed, hydrated, or even completely tested or tested accurately. They'd walk off mid-way through a test and go who knows where and not come back for an hour. The torment and torture I speak of is real and it is done by human hands. Hands connected to bodies whose thoughts are of neglect and cruelty, not for the comforting of human souls and the healing of their bodies and minds. Emotions such as love, kindness and humility were on a far distant shore this morning, for they certainly did not exist in the emergency room.

    This ER was my new, albeit temporary home. All because of one test whose readings came back wrong. My electrolytes however, proved to be fine. I could have and should have been transferred up to the psych ward at any time after I was admitted. However I was not.

    As things turned out, it would seem to everything, even to misery there is a purpose. God's plan must play out. From six in the morning until six at night I laid there next to the nurses station, underneath an impossibly bright light. This was a spot where I had ample view to see and hear a great deal of nothing happening. It was also a place where I could hear a great deal of suffering by my fellow patients. One of which was right behind me. I could not see her, but I most certainly could hear her. She truly was a character, but kindred in nature. At this time I had no idea what lay in store for me, nor that this person would play such a big part in what was to come. All I knew was that I was afraid of the future. I did not know what was wrong with me or what it would take to get me back to something close to normalcy. Nor did I know how long it would take, or if I'd have to stay in the psych ward for days, weeks or months. All I knew was that I was panicking and scared, and that the future seemed a long way off.

Chapter 1.
Non-Emergency.

Recalling the first twelve hours of my stay in the emergency room is like sitting on a porcupine. The act is something best left undone. For the sake of this memoir my memories must surface, albeit temporarily, if only to record them for posterity. Even though I was there a relatively short amount of time, a great deal occurred during those hours. Of all things, nothing and nobody was more dreaded, almost hated than my nurse, whom I shall refer to as Adam. A pseudonym, of course. Adam was the worst nurse imaginable. That he has employment in a hospital casts a dark shadow over the entire complex. He is a living, walking, talking curse to all whom fall under his care.

My first encounter with Adam was when he came up to my bedside with a blood pressure machine. What his intentions were and what I thought they were going to be were two entirely different things. Adam wrapped my arm up and I sat there connected to the little machine and walked away. I sat a little longer and then sat a lot longer. Adam had started the machine up and simply disappeared. He never returned to check the results. I was simply left sitting there with this Velcro strap around my arm. It was up to me to check the readings and then disengage myself from the device. Hours would pass and the machine sat next to me without an owner. Such are first impressions. This nurse who had been assigned to me was terrible and derelict in his duties.

By this time I had reclaimed my voice, if not my ability to walk. Thus, from time to time I would ask a passerby where my nurse was, and whomever it was that I had stopped stated that they would try to find him. Indeed, perhaps they did. However, that did not stop Adam from remaining MIA. When he finally did resurface assistance would be directly asked for, a promise would be given and nothing would come of it. I was left to languish without access to food or drink or decent toilet facilities for most of the time I spent in the ER. There was a bathroom nearby, but nobody to help me out of the bed to get there. When I eventually reclaimed my ability to walk and got myself into the bathroom, a monumental feets, it was dirty, unkempt and it offered very little in the way of paper towels and no toilet paper. I literally had to steal some toilet paper from off a nearby cart before I could use the facility. As for Adam, the term liar could be offered up here, but that would suppose that there was any amount of truth in this lifeform to begin with. There wasn't. He could not tell the truth nor perform his duties as a nurse with any iota of tender compassion. His only goal seemed to be to avoid his patients and not have them intrude upon his day. All the while the patients in the ER were left to fend for themselves in between being taken for tests and speaking with a doctor. A nurse, Adam might have been, but nursing was not within his capabilities. Without a proper nurse, I was left alone to fend for myself.

    The hours would pass slowly, ever so slowly with nothing to do, nobody to talk to and an ever increasing sense of terror creeping up within me. Literally, nothing happened to me. I simply sat under an impossibly bright fluorescent light all morning and afternoon with nothing better to do than listen to patients come and go. Some, rather quickly I'd say, which I must say made me envious. They retreated to their loved ones whereas I was allowed no phone, no television, no radio, no video games and no books. It was just me and my anxiety disorder all to our lonesome. To this very day I see no reason for taking a psychiatric patients phone away while they are still in the emergency room. At the very least a phone would give them a connection to family and friends, as well as something to occupy the hours of solitude. Leaving one with nothing only makes a condition worse, and worse I became. Slowly I fell, as I was suffocating for companionship and kindness in a ward filled with people.

    My mother would arrive within the first hours of my stay and offer the companionship needed. However, there was nothing to do and I was apparently going nowhere anytime soon. I did not want her to suffer the tedium of the ER, and so I told her she could go home. There was nothing she could do here. I appreciated her company more than I could ever tell her, but the ER was a place of misery and I wanted to spare her my fate. She left, and it would be at the twelfth hour mark of my stay before another diversion of sorts was offered. That would make the time around 6:00pm, or so. I do not remember the exact time, only that it was at about this time that an impossible-to-ignore event occurred. A woman, fifty-ish or so had arrived in the emergency room. She came with lungs a blazing. Screaming, hollering, yelling, all of these are accurate descriptions of her lone activity, and she was ablaze with fury the entirety of her time spent in the ER. Which, mercifully for me was a short spell. After twelve hours of neglect and increasingly volatile panic attacks, I was in no condition to handle the sound of unending arguments between doctor and patient, occurring directly behind me, no less.

    Being in a semi-conscious state at the time, I do not have a full recollection of what was said between the woman and her new friendly doctor. What I do remember is faint, and most likely due to my discussions with this woman in the days ahead as we became friends in the psych ward. I remember, more or less, what she told me about her time in the ER, and that was quite a bit. At this moment she was simply a woman I could not see, yet even so I could certainly sense her presence. One that was, by the tone and volume of her voice, distressed, and with cause. The woman, whom I shall call Gail, had been forcibly picked up by EMT's after her family reported a Facebook post which they claimed indicated that Gail suffered from suicidal ideations. To this day I do not know if this claim was justified. Through my talks with Gail I came to understand that her family believed it was true, and because of their belief Gail was brought into the ER as a suicide risk. That meant that Gail had to go the psych ward. There were no if's, and's or buts. She had to go up for seventy-two hours of observation, which she most certainly did not want to do. This was a desire that Gail made repeatedly over the course of her hour long stay in the ER. Gail did not want to go to the psych ward, nor did she want to remain in the hospital at all. She wanted to go home. As a woman who had done nothing wrong Gail felt it was her right to stand up and walk out of the hospital whenever she so desired. However, the report had been made and she had to be held for the mandatory observation period, if only to see if her families claim had any merit. Thus, the hostile argument continued on and on, circular sentiments repeating over and over again. I do recall the mention of cigarettes being made. As a former smoker myself, I remember thinking I could use a smoke myself. It was unfortunate for Gail and I that the hospital is a non-smoking campus, so neither of us were allowed to go out and light one up. This too was a cause of much grief for both Gail and the doctor overseeing her case. For Gail did not like hearing the word no. It was the trigger word that restarted whatever argument was currently in progress. Those arguments came fast and furious.

In the end, due to the continued protestation of the medical staff and the pleading of her family, Gail allowed herself to be committed. Her case was most amazing to me. Not that Gail had caved in so relatively quickly, but the speed with which she was transferred upstairs to the psych ward. No sooner did she give her consent than she was being wheeled out of the ER and up to the second floor. Whereas I, having been there for thirteen hours and growing increasingly despondent and depressed, was left to suffer alone. Something definitely felt wrong, and the incoherency of my thought processes at this time always directed inward. I felt something was wrong with me and it was why I was being abandoned hour after hour. In the mind of someone under mental duress, logic is not applicable. Whatever is thought to be true is true. Regardless of how nonsensical the thought may be.

What happened next was symbolic of my entire time in the ER. A meal was finally served to me. If one could in any feasible way call what was on my tray as being fit for human consumption, that is. My nurse, Adam, did not make the meal any more appetizing than it looked. He referred to it as dog food. Which is truly what the meat portion of the meal looked like. It resembled something that had been dumped out of a can of Alpo. The meal consisted of some kind of meat that was sliced and sauced, along with some water and apple juice. Not having eaten for twenty-four hours, I ate. Not that I was so much concerned with aesthetics as I was with having something to do. Eating was a distraction from my circumstances, which were growing increasingly worse by the hour. My thoughts became more confused. My fear rose to levels I'd never known before. Not that I was afraid of anything or anyone in particular, I was afraid of everything and everyone around me. Panic flooded my brain. Life was miserable.

Things seemed to grow darker by the hour. However, a small light was seen at the end of the tunnel. A long way off, but it was seen. The physician who reviews electrolyte anomalies entered the ER and found that my test had been in error. My electrolytes were fine. I was immediately cleared to be transferred out of the ER and up to the psych ward. As I've already stated, this was only hour thirteen of the eighteen hours I called this hell home. His clearance was overlooked and I was left to sit in the ER for five more hours, awaiting a rooms availability in the floors above me. Purpose, to be cleared for the psych ward a second time. This was incompetence on fine display.

Those next five hours came at a heavy personal cost and removed what light there was within my field of vision. Cloaked was I, within a darkness deeper than the forest on a moonless night. A shadowed cover unequal to the night previous nor covering the span of my entire life. I was soon to be stuck in a panic attack that would not end. Nobody, and I repeat nobody seemed to be able to help me. Nobody even came to try.

Try to imagine being frightened, cornered, trapped and alone in a depressing black room. There is nobody around and nothing can be heard but the sound of your own inner voice telling you that you are not safe. This was me on the night of the second of November, 2023.

It was a little past seven p.m. And it was now my turn to scream and to holler and to yell at the top of my lungs. I spoke one word and that word was help. Repeatedly and with increasing volume I pleaded for help. I was terrified and out of my head, incapable of speaking more than this one lonely word. I knew I needed help and needed it now and nobody was coming. No nurse, no doctor, no other patient. Nobody. I was totally alone. The only point at which my existence was acknowledged was when I tried to leave my bed and escape the hospital. I was in turn locked into my bed so I could not leave. After this action I was abandoned again, this time for five hours.

At about midnight something happened. I do not know what, but my anguished pleas for assistance were answered. Not in the way I expected. I was not taken to the psych ward. I was transferred to the general part of the hospital where they treat patients with physical problems. My short-term residence was a room shared with another, but it was away from the insane cruelty of the ER. I had a team of nurses around me, a TV, a phone and a bed. Being mentally and physically exhausted, I crashed into the bed provided to me and offered up a prayer of Thanksgiving. Perhaps not verbally but from my heart. I thanked The Lord that I was no longer in that hellish creation of mankind that now lay beneath me. A structure with loneliness, abandonment and fear as its foundation. It was as if my life, as if my very humanity were irrelevant within those walls. I did not know what was ahead or what awaited me in the psych ward, but somehow I knew that it would not be as bad as what I'd just lived through. Time would prove me right. The immediate future was not as bad, but there were a few moments when it came oh so close.

Chapter 2.
Friday, November 3rd, 2023.

Awakening to find myself in a proper hospital room, my stay in my relative room of luxury was brief. Twelve hours to be exact. Perhaps this rest period was given to me via an act of divine intervention. A time and place given that I might stabilize and relax. To get my bearings, if you will. I most certainly needed a moment to chill after the night of terror I'd just suffered in the ER. My stay was in this room was not perfect. I was given zero medication, neither for physical nor mental problems, and only one quick visit with a staff psychiatrist, so my mental state was somewhere between conscious thought and depression. Even so, I was able to sleep a few hours and awaken with the rising sun.

When I found myself awake and alert I was not rested mind you, just aware of what was around me. Try to imagine for a moment receiving an electric shock. The moment of contact is incredibly painful. The moments afterward are more or less spent in a stupor. Thought, while possible is not probable. To put it frankly, all I did was stare at the television and whatever channels came in clearly. It certainly was amazing that even in this day of digital television where we should get picture perfect reception, a hospital could still get cable TV with static filled channels. I'd not seen that in many a year. Even with the TV reception being what it was, I can say it was a pleasant diversion. As was my breakfast. At the very least I was able to get a good meal in me before being transferred on toward the psych ward. Thank goodness the meal was nothing like what I was served the night before in the ER. A stomach can only handle so much suffering. I was pleasantly surprised to find that was I able to order some scrambled eggs and toast with coffee. It was not a large breakfast, but it was filling. Along with a pleasant chat with my roommate while we ate, the dawning of a new day proved to be most pleasant and restful.

My roommate was a kind, gentle, elderly fellow who must have been in his seventies. He was a jolly guy who was filled with words of wisdom and many fascinating stories. Which is good news for me because I still wasn't talking much and didn't have all that much to contributed to a conversation. My roommate was quite content to do all of the talking. Odd, when I think about him after all this time. Twenty-four hours earlier I'd been alone and scared. With the birth of a new day I was comfortable and had company. If time had permitted I would have enjoyed speaking with this man in more detail, or at least listening to what he had to say. That was not to be. Just as soon as I was transferred into his room I was taken out of it. About midnight I arrived and around noon I departed. In so short a time I was to discover the difference between the recuperative part of the hospital and the psych ward. What a difference it was, indeed.

A nurse came to pick me up and I was transported from one unit to another via wheelchair. Upon arriving into the psych ward both nurse and chair departed and I was alone with two women who turned out to be support staff for the unit. They weren't medically trained but they still helped oversee the unit. Upon entry into what would be my private room, at least for a time, I was left speechless. Everything that I had enjoyed in my shared hospital room was stripped from me. Everything but a bed, a pillow and two blankets. The bed, having a paper thin mattress was nothing to write home about. The television, the phone, immediate access to a nurse and any wall decor was painfully absent from the room I was placed in. In short, I was provided the bare minimum. The bed, a table and as shelf for my things. Otherwise, the white room was as vacant as it was large, cold and empty. If you would picture a Summer camp lodging, one big room, spacious, with nothing but a two rows of beds and a shared table. This room is only lit by the dim light of the moon. That is what I was given. Only instead of fifteen beds for the campers, there were two, and there was nobody to talk to. The second bed was currently unoccupied and would remain so for the majority of my stay. The sight before me was a shock to be sure and took time to get used to. As did the dim glow offered by the rooms light fixture.

At first I thought I had been placed in an unused storage room. I always thought a psych ward room would be just like any other hospital room I'd stayed in over the course of my life, possessing the usual accoutrements associated with a hospital. A heart monitor, a hook for fluids to be hung on, perhaps an intercom system and video cameras. There would be something, anything that would indicate that this was indeed a hospital room. Yet the room was cold, silent and empty. All the room truly offered was a singular window with a view of the part of the hospital I'd just been taken from, as well as the goings on outside on the street below. The room, my room, taken in full was a depressing sight and experience. However, as I'd come to learn there was good cause for the room being as it was. Nothing else was needed.

Most of the patients who entered the psych ward needed very little. A bed, five blankets and a pillow, as well as access to the rooms adjoining bathroom. For many, that's all they needed. Once the patients were given their medication all they did was sleep. All day, all night, passed or through mealtime, they slept. I was the exception. The insomniac who couldn't sleep more than a few hours a day, if that. It was therefore my pleasure to have a big two-bed psych ward room all to my insomniac self. From nine at night until seven in the morning the room was mine and I had two choices. I could either lay in bed and pretend to rest or get up and look out the window, which I must point out was the coldest spot in the room. There was a third option, although I did not know it that first night. Yet it proved to be just as lonesome as staying in my room. We, as patients were allowed out of our rooms at night if we desired to walk the one one long hallway that made up the majority of the psych ward. This was the one nighttime activity that was allowed. The hallway challenge. Simply put, we were allowed to see how many times we could walk from one end of the hallway to the other end and return. Thirty times? Sixty times? It didn't really matter how often you did it. This was a matter of a personal nature. This was an activity to keep patients expending energy and focused on trivialities until the doctors were back in the building. Of course, on those rare occasions when two people were awake at the same time during those wee morning hours, there would be someone to talk to. For a little while, anyway. They'd soon go back to bed and it was back to the long, silent, solitary walk that lay before me.

The nurses were at their station. Physicians were on call but absent. The psychiatrists had all gone home for the evening. The patients, they were mostly asleep. For an insomniac at night, a psych ward can be a truly lonely place. Were it not for the huge office clock as seen through the reception window, there would have been no way to note the passage of time. That clock was a friend to many. Every tick it tocked was one second closer to freedom, and home. Such are first impressions.

After being given the customary introduction to the psych ward, medical papers were given to me and I was subjected to a strip search. This was to be the most interaction I had with the psych ward staff during my entire stay in the hospital. For interactions with employees, caretakers if you will, were kept to a minimum. After it was found that I was not trying to sneak any contraband into the psych ward, I was left on my own in my great big cold room. Were it not for the Bible that my mom had brought me I'd truly have been all alone. While it was not the only book in the psych ward, The Holy Scriptures were all that was present that would offer any measure of comforting. Having that book lay on my heart offered me what I was getting nowhere else. The presence of The Bible made me feel as if God were with me. Otherwise, on that first day, I sat there alone in my room, wide-eyed, scared and awake with my bible in my arms. Slowly, I turned page after page all the while wondering what lay around me. After reading a few chapters I decided to go to the one place where I knew I'd find some level of escape. The TV room. A humble setting which doubled as the psych ward cafeteria. For a TV addict like myself I knew I could find some escape from my surroundings in the grainy pictures emanating from the television set hanging on the wall. Thankfully, the television was still there. Someone had tried to punch a hole into the enclosure that surrounded the television. As was evidenced by the damage done to the metal frame which stood as a barrier between the patients and the television. Otherwise the room was unremarkable. Painted white, there were scant Halloween decorations still on the walls. Undoubtably created by past occupants of the ward. There were many long white tables and blue plastic chairs, all identical. For someone suffering a rectal tear like myself, the plastic chairs were incredibly uncomfortable, yet I somehow found a away to make due. After all, this was the only place where I could watch television. I certainly suffered for the opportunity to have my beloved TV back. Otherwise, a few old books sat long unread next to a few boxes filled with puzzle pieces. Pieces which had obviously been put together many times, as evidenced by the absence of so many pieces. There was also a box of crayons and some coloring sheets provided for amusement. As time would pass a few decks of cards would be added to the routine, but at this point the cards were a gift still left ungiven. Sparse hardly defines this rooms entertainment possibilities. Depressing would be a more accurate term. The TV was the center of attention, at least for me. Fortunately, nobody else was around who wanted to watch television, and so I had the remote to myself. Yet, even though the TV was mine I was not alone. There was a woman in the room with me. Small, petite, blonde and in her thirties, I'd guess, she sat in a wheel-chair while working on a puzzle. I shall call her Amanda.

Amanda was nice, talkative and polite. After introducing herself she invited me to sit with her. I took her up on her invitation. I soon learned that Amanda was in the process of being discharged. Here I was having just arrived and there she was, waiting on her ride home. We were two strangers passing in the night, as it were. This proved to be a fortunate meeting. Amanda, having been in the psych ward for a while, I don't know how long, she knew the ins and outs of the unit. What to do and what not to do. What to say and what not to say. Amanda gave me the low down on how to get out of the psych ward quickly. Her biggest piece of advice was that if I wanted to be discharged fast, just keep my mouth shut and do whatever I was told. If I were respectful and quiet I'd be getting out soon. If I caused a fuss or talked back to staff, I could expect a longer stay. I took everything she said to heart and remembered each and every word during my stay.

Being discharged, Amanda no longer had need of some of the things she'd been given while a patient. One item in particular was an empty notebook that came with a little pencil. Little did she know what this gift would mean to me and enable me to do. This generous offering was a gesture most precious, and one that I will always treasure. For her gift got me to do something I'd not done for months. That would be write. While in the psych ward I began working on a collection of poems reflecting my thoughts during the days of my confinement, as well as immediately following my release. Eventually, those poems became a series of books and all were published. From Amanda's gift came so much good. My physical health and my mental state improved due to the therapeutic value of writing. Within a year I'd release six books of poems, all because of a chance meeting and a gift given to me by a stranger. I owe much to this young woman whom I only met one time and talked with for an hour. I will always be grateful to her.

At this point I would be remiss if I did not mention what was at the other end of the hallway. For on one end of the psych ward was the freezing cold TV room which seemed incapable of being heated. This was the room where I spent my days. At the other end of the long corridor was another TV room. It was well heated, had several cushioned sofas and was always occupied when open. Why not spend my time in a place where I'd be warm and where there was a second TV, not to mention people to talk to? The answer is simple. The TV didn't work. It was stuck on the same opening screen most of the time. There was one patient who seemed to have knowledge of how to change the station, but that darn TV would always revert back to the welcome screen. Minus a television, all that room offered was silence, sofa's and heat. This is where many of the patients slept throughout the day. It was the only place in the psych ward in which to keep warm. For one who actually wanted to watch television, I suffered the cold by myself at the other end of the hallway and was just grateful for what I had. That being Comedy Central, South Park and Seinfeld. I was in pain, cold and still suffering from insomnia but at least I had television. At least that old friend was still there.

After Amanda's departure I eventually returned to my room. Time passed slowly but soon it was long passed dark and time for lights out. I would not meet my psychiatrist until the morning, so this night I was not only off my normal medications, but not on anything new either. This was the eternal night that dragged on from lights out until breakfast time when once again the TV room would be opened, and I would be fed. I was to be awake, alone and bored for hours. However, I felt safe. At least I was in a place where I would eventually find the help I needed, and I believed this. The help would not be found this night, for certain, but I knew it would be coming. Waiting was the hard part. Especially during the silent, starlit hours just before dawn.

Chapter 3.
Saturday, November 4th, 2023.

My memories regarding my first full day as a psych ward patient are sparse. Perhaps due to extreme fatigue, or simply there might not be all that much to remember. Whatever might be the cause, I recall very little from that time. Arising long before sunrise, I did not even know when breakfast was going to be served. I would have to wait until someone was in the hallway whom I could ask. I was lethargic, a little on edge and I was lonely. I missed my cats more than anything in the world. I remember thinking to myself I've only been in this hospital for two days yet it felt so much longer. It felt as if I'd been away from my beloved pets for a month. I did not realize how much I relied upon them for my day to day emotional wellbeing up until I was away from them for an extended period of time. Now that I was without them, a big part of me was missing. I knew they were being well cared for by family and friends. Even so, I wanted to be with them desperately.

Upon learning that breakfast would be served at eight and that the TV room would open at seven, I simply waited outside the darkened doorway that separated me from the television, and food. Wide eyed and awake, I waited. I stood in silence, longing for the morning television news and whatever would be my first meal in this new place. Fate, it appears, was by my side. For once the TV room was opened and I was able to pull up a chair and watch TV, it was not long before another patient wandered in, half asleep, disheveled and somewhat grouchy. Most definitely, she was hungry. I knew the moment she opened her mouth who it was. It was Gail. There are oh so few individuals in this entire world that have a voice like hers. I could pick her rough tones out of a thousand persons. Her voice was older yet still feminine, only combined with a roughness that comes with drug abuse and age. Also, her time using drugs had robbed her of her teeth, and she was having trouble getting someone to bring her her dentures. Heavy-set but not obese, she stood about five foot two. Gail's hair was brownish in color combined with a tinge of gray. I knew right away that this was most certainly the woman who was behind me in the ER, having been sent up well before me. She'd been in the psych ward a day longer than myself and that spell of twenty-four hours had quieted her down considerably. She did not have much to say as we met face to face. A sparsely filled room occupied by strangers, there wasn't much too say. Barely anyone was fully awake and most looked like I felt. Abandoned, alone and depressed. Gail, in particular looked despondent. Having been in this unit longer than myself, Gail more than likely had already seen her psychiatrist. Gail's depleted energy very well may have been due to a medication adjustment or addition. Or, more likely, she was detoxing off of her street drug of choice. Maybe it was a combination of these factors which was responsible for her mellowness. Whatever the case may be she was looking for a friend. She needed someone to listen to her tale and that person wound up being me. Perhaps this was in part due to there being nobody else around, the choices were slim. However, I was glad to have someone to talk to during those first few days I spent in the psych ward. Gail was a kindred spirit and a very kind soul.

As I listened to Gail talk about her life, her problems and what she was currently facing I began to realize how wonderful I had it in life. I may not have been at my mental tip-top, but I did have a home, my animals, my mother and a good support system waiting for me on the outside. Even though I felt alone I was in fact very blessed. Regarding Gail, what I increasingly became aware of is that she currently had nothing and nobody. All she possessed were the clothes on her back provided by the hospital as well as the clothes she arrived in. Her family had abandoned her to the doctors, nurses and staff of the psych ward on the spot. As frightened as I was in this place at least I knew I'd be getting out and going home to family and friends. I did not know when but I knew that at some point I'd be going home. Gail, on the other hand, learned by silence the state of her current affairs. A call home was rejected. The psych wards phone number, it had been blocked. Her daughter had essentially disowned her. Gail really was alone. As her new friend I could not offer her much, but I did offer her my sympathy and emotional support. I listened to her sorrow on a daily basis, as well as whatever few family updates came her way. They were indeed few and slow in coming.

During those first days in the psych ward there was routine. That routine involved Gail and I sitting in that cold TV room, or at times in the warmer room down the hall, chit-chatting about our lives, what we'd been through and how we ended up where we currently resided. Gail's story, as best as I can recall, her time in the psych ward was due to a poorly worded Facebook post. The night of her commitment she had made a post that read along the lines of she'd rather be dead than have tolerate something or other. I don't know what that something was. Her family reported Gail's post to the police department as a family member in suicidal distress. Although she had been taken to the emergency room against her will, she had ultimately agreed to be committed. A topic I will touch on later in this book. Whether or not Gail actually meant what she posted, that indeed she was suicidal, or if hers were simply a poor choice of words, this is not for me to judge. However in all the talks I had with Gail, not once did she ever wish for her demise or make any threats to that effect. I suspect that there was far more to the situation than I was made aware of, but I did not press. If she did not wish to talk of it then it wasn't my business to know. What Gail did relate is that she'd had a heated argument with her daughter in which Gail's phone got destroyed, by Gail herself, and that argument was why her daughter would not talk to her. I encouraged Gail to keep reaching out, trying the phone number and seeing if it would eventually become unblocked. Try each day and try to get through. Until then, work with the social worker that everyone was supposed to see just in case she needed a place to stay when she was discharged. Not so great advice on my part, at least in regards to the social worker. I never met the woman myself. I saw her talking with other people, but I never had the pleasure of an introduction. Perhaps it was decided I did not need the extra support, I do not know. I'm not sure Gail ever talked to her either. She might have, I simply don't know. The social worker was overworked and had a constant stream of new patients to deal with. She also had her hands full with some really problematic patients. Perhaps not seeing her was an indication that I was not as bad off as I thought. Whatever the case may be, I encouraged Gail to try to talk to the social worker and get some suggestions on where she could rent a cheap place, fast. In 2023, that was not an easy task to accomplish, regardless if you were a psych ward patient or just a regular fellow on the street. Apartments were expensive. This was a pressing problem for Gail but not an immediate one. She still had several days to go before she could feasibly be discharged. Until that time we both waited and prayed.

    There is one memory of Gail that I would like to recount, only in that it was so incredibly strange and unique to her alone and it has to do with meals. Everyone in the psych ward ordered their own food. There was quite a choice of breakfasts, lunches and dinners to choose from on the menu provided to us. We did not starve. The food was good, not great but not bad. It was okay. For my part, the constant stress I'd been under had made chewing incredibly difficult, as I was clenching my teeth a lot during these stress filled days and nights. My left jaw was not working properly. There was a feeling of crunching whenever I opened and closed my jaw, and I would hear a clicking sound too. Eating was difficult and sometimes painful. I must say that stress wreaks havoc on the body in the most peculiar of ways. Ultimately, this was a matter that eventually needed the attention of a dentist. He would prescribed a night guard to keep me from grinding my teeth in my sleep. Once I had received my night guard, my jaw clenching subsided rather quickly. That was not to be of any assistance during my stay in the psych ward. I had to eat small bites and chew very carefully. Even so, I will say that the food we were served was good, and Gail received a lot of it. I do not know why and I may never know why, but most of us received a regular serving size of whatever we had ordered. Gail, on the other hand received a tray loaded from top to bottom and side to side, three times a day no less. She couldn't eat it all! Nobody could eat it all! It was simply too much food for one person to digest. This regular occurrence was a source of great amusement in what was otherwise a dreary setting.

    Three times a day those who could would gather for their meals. This ward had about thirty-four beds, maybe more. Yet at meal time there were around ten people partaking in the feast. It didn't matter if the unit were nearing capacity or only had a handful of humans residing in it, meal time was not a social occasion. People would enter, get their food, eat and leave and then return to their rooms to sleep. Gail and I, along with one or two others were the only ones who would speak to each other. The rest seemed to be in a drugged stupor, eating out of habit but not hunger. Some even trying to stay awake as they chewed their food. I'm not really sure what more one would expect in a psych ward during supper time, although I was soon to find out.

One other item of note. There always seemed to be a plentiful supply of decaffeinated coffee and ice water on hand. We had to ask for it of course, as we had to ask for anything that was needed. Shampoo, toothbrushes, tooth paste, soap, razors, shaving cream, towels, blankets, new clothes, whatever we needed would be supplied upon request. Coffee was an outside pleasure we all looked forward to. The cups weren't large and it wasn't Starbucks, but it was coffee and it was hot. Which, in this place that was so often so very cold, anything warm to drink was readily welcomed by all present.

My first full day in the psych ward proved not to be bad, just sedate. I of course saw my psychiatrist first thing in the morning and he began to put me back on some of my regular medications. He also started me on a new medication which I'd never been on before. It was something to help me sleep, as well as keep me from being so very awake, alert and anxious at all times. He put me on Doxepin. Ten MG's three times a day and then a much larger dosage at night. I didn't know what to expect with this new medication other than it was supposed to make me sleepy. Time proved that it did. After a full day of listening to Gail's many issues and eating more than I'd eaten in over a month, I was indeed sleepy, and as I placed my head upon my pillow I did something that I'd not done in well over a month. I went right to sleep. From 10:00pm until about 6:00 a.m. the following morning I was in dreamland. This was a slumber that was much needed and most welcome.

Chapter 4.
Monday, November 6th, 2023.

Upon my initial entry into the psych ward, one of the first things that Amanda advised me to do was to do whatever was asked of me. Just do it, like the old commercial said. Don't complain, don't argue. Just do it. The more you talk back the worse it will be for you, because the medical staff knows everything that goes on in the unit. One of the things that we all had to partake in was group therapy. However, the first few days of my confinement were on the weekend, and because of this there were few activities planned. Events consisted of coloring, writing, talking and television, as well as putting the pieces of my mind back together while working on the various puzzles which were in the TV room. Yet, no therapy was offered. The weekends, as Amanda had explained to me earlier, were boring. She was right. The weekends were indeed boring. Not entirely so, but for the most part there was little to occupy the mind.

To break the monotony of each day, patients were offered the kindness of two women who'd been working in the mental health system for many years. Each came into the psych ward to play games, play music on their phones, as well as run an arts and crafts program. Their visits were activity filled festivals where we could color with markers, make bracelets with beads, or play games of UNO. Then there was a mock game of Jeopardy. I was awful at everything. My creativeness does not stretch to making things with my hands. With that having being said, I don't know what the psychological advantage of bracelet making might be, but I still have the two bracelets I made. They are on display in my living room. Their monetary value is zero, but there is a certain sentimental attachment I have to them that I cannot explain. Perhaps it's just as simple as any act of kindness during a crisis is appreciated, and I like to remember those times, for even if one is not good at it arts and crates are fun to do. The creative process offers a chance to get in out of the coldness of the regular psych ward and enjoy a well heated room and have some fun while listening to music. That's what these excursions amounted too. A chance to stop thinking about being a psychiatric patient and do something normal. Something besides eat and sleep, that is. Heaven knows there was ample enough opportunity for those two activities while I was there.

As for what officially counted as group therapy and what had to be attended, that was something else entirely. We never really knew when they would descend upon us, although we had a general idea of time of day. Yet, I think I can sum up group therapy in the words of one of my fellow patients as we saw that incredible mass come strolling down the hallway one day. "Oh, Hell no!"

Group therapy was run by a doctor of some sort, I'll say that much. However her participation was minimal. For the most part, the doctor got the event started and put and end to it. The time in between, which usually ran about an hour, consisted of medical students who were getting a taste of what it was like to work among psychiatric patients. These future psychiatrists were to play games with us and reward us with candy and paper achievement awards. The games were pretty basic, sometimes Bingo, a game which was played until everyone reached a Bingo. Nobody was a loser. Then there was a game where a ball was thrown around the room, and the beach ball had a great deal of writing on it. When you caught the ball you looked under your hand and saw what you had to reveal about yourself. The revelations were nothing majorly dramatic, more like a basic coverage of events. The who, what, why, where and when of why you were in the psych ward. We'd throw the ball around and whomever caught it had to answer the question. All in all it felt more like we were being studied rather than treated. Which is one of the reasons my fellow patient vocalized the "Oh, Hell no." At times their attention was far too much.

All in all I will say this. The group therapy sessions did serve a purpose. If not an intended one. It helped those in the psych ward get to know each other a little better. We had to reveal our personal feelings and inner selves, things not usually revealed to total strangers. As a result of the revelations I remember thinking to myself that what I'm going through is small potatoes compared to what my fellow patients were living through. The drug abuse, the physical illnesses, the familial estrangement that they suffered put me in my place. Then there were the patients who'd been so tortured by society that there was virtually nothing left of them mentally, physically or emotionally. I learned all too quickly that nobody was committed to the psych ward by accident. Of course there are stories of such things in the news, corrupt doctors abusing the system and all that jazz. However, from what I could tell from my time among the other patients was that everyone was there for a reason. That reason being we all needed help. Some more than others, however everyone needed something that they weren't getting before they entered the hospital.

I cannot remember which night it was for certain. Perhaps Monday, however I honestly do not know. Up until the hour in question my stay in the psych ward had been uneventful. Boring, even. I'd wake up in the morning, eat breakfast and watch TV. I'd then partake in whatever activities were planned for the day. Otherwise, it was get medicated and watch television. This particular night however was different. For the first time since I was removed from the emergency room I would feel frightened, terrified even. I was forced into a state of mind where I was unsure of the reality of my surroundings and my ability to survive in them. For the next two days this would be a constant state of fear which I would have to adapt to. A new patient had been admitted into the psych ward during the midnight hour, and because many of us slept with our doors open in order to get heat into our rooms, we were vulnerable. This new patient, one whom I shall refer to as Tom, immediately proved why he was placed among us, and I was the first to receive the revelation. For I woke up that night and found him in my bathroom, using the facility to relieve himself. Let me make this clear, patients are not to be in others patients room, ever. Yet there he was, in mine, while I was asleep. At first I was unsure if I were dreaming or not. A nightmare about my surroundings and about my commitment. Only this was no night terror, it was really happening. Tom arose from his throne and left my room and returned to his own. I called out after him and one of the staff came running into the hallway. He said he was aware of Tom and that this event would not happen again. Some things cannot be controlled or guaranteed, and the same can be for people. Especially in a ward filled with mental patients. The staff member was wrong. It did happen again and with its occurrence came a major setback in the precarious state of my mental well-being.

Coloring during Arts & Crafts.

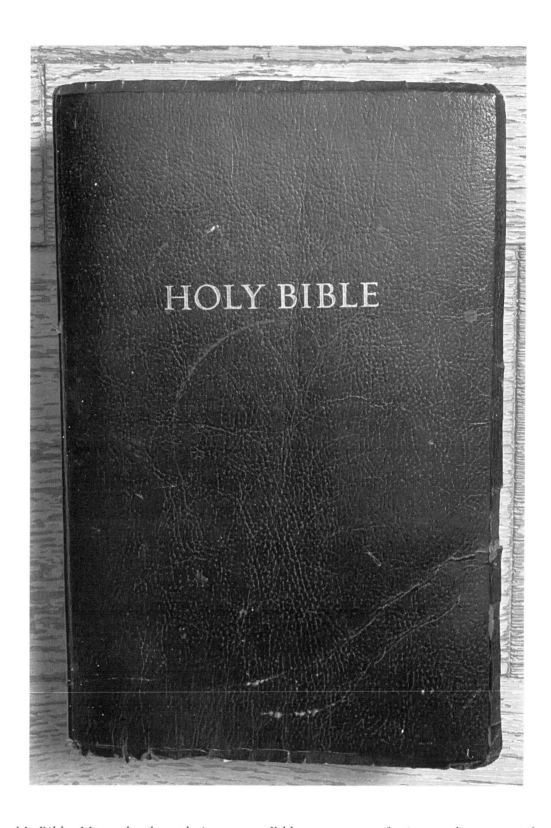

My Bible. My mother brought it to me so I'd have some comforting reading material.

One of the bracelets I made during Arts & Crafts.

Another bracelet I made. This one resembling a rosary.

A drawing I made, using dominos I'd found laying on a table.

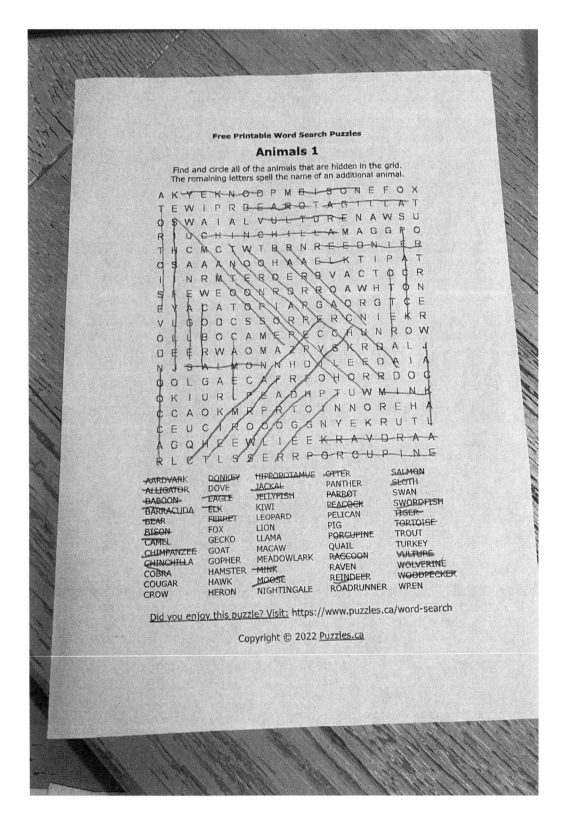

One of the many word searches I did during my stay.

A game of Bingo where everyone wins.

An award for existing.

Coloring has always been a favorite passtime!

This kitty had white fur.

Chapter 5.
Monday, November 6th, 2023.

Around 5:00pm on Monday afternoon several patients were gathered in the TV room / cafeteria having yet another quiet supper. Everyone who I was accustomed to seeing there was present. Myself, Gail, a young man whom I learned was suffering a brain tumor, another who was detoxing of off illegal drugs, and a woman whom I suspect had been in the ward for quite some time. However, one person was conspicuous by his absence. Tom. I thought little of his absence, and was in fact grateful for the peace of mind this brought to me. It is a fact that new patients often miss meals in the psych ward. It often takes them a few days to get adjusted to whatever drugs they are put on, or are coming off of. They sleep twenty-four hours a day for days on end. If only I'd been so fortunate in regards to Tom. When Tom presented himself ten minutes into our meal, I had a sense that something was amiss. I cannot remember what gave me this impression. Perhaps it was a particular demeanor Tom carried or his crooked smile, but something about him was off. More so than usual. It was not until after I finished my meal and returned to my room that I found out what had delayed Tom. As I entered my bathroom to brush my teeth I saw the disaster that lay before me. In my absence Tom had entered my room and defecated all over the bathroom toilet. I shall spare all of the gruesome details, but Tom had left a vile mess never before seen by my eyes.

    I knew who had violated my space, only I did not know why. Flashbacks to my childhood and a time of being bullied quickly surfaced. The years and years of elementary school torment that had been placed upon me by my peers. Transferring from one school to another to escape the threat of violence, only to find it once again in a new setting. Now, here I was as an adult having come full circle. Someone had targeted me. They'd acted on their malicious desires twice in less than twenty-four hours. My response was all it could have been at that stage of my mental illness, a return to youth. Seek out someone in charge and let them know. Mentally, I was ten years old once more and looking for someone older, wiser, and stronger to protect me. Only there weren't too many older people on staff at night. I was left to tell a woman I shall call Betty, who seemed to be the boss among all the non-medical staff. I found Betty, still in the TV room tending to the patients and their suppers. I told Betty what I had discovered and events progressed from there. My wish was that Betty would somehow magically make the situation less frightening. I don't know how exactly but I desperately hoped for the alleviation of my mounting anxiety. Escape was coming, but a rocky road lay before me before I found myself free of fear.

After Betty made a quick inspection of the damage done to my bathroom she was direct in her response. She sought out Tom in the TV room, only he had left that location as soon as I had reentered. Tom had returned to his own room. Betty tracked him down to that location and immediately demanded that he clean up the mess he had made in my bathroom. Tom, apparently furious that he'd been told on, stormed off into my bathroom and cleaned up the fecal matter he had deposited all over my toilet. After which, Tom returned to his room. This response on Betty's part might have been sufficient had I been in my right mind. However, I was not. Long forgotten childhood trauma combined with present events triggered and unleashed all of the fear and insecurity pent up within my mind. I began to cocoon once again, in the same fashion that had necessitated my entry into the psych ward in the first place. At first it was a slow decent. However the longer the trigger remained present the quicker the cocooning enveloped me.

I must pause here for clarification on my condition. At the time that these events were taking place, the doctors thought I suffered from catatonia. That was not the case. After a great deal of intensive therapy I've learned what I experienced and still experience is more of a mental wrap around my memories and my sense of self. My personal identity, if you will. That which makes me who I am ceases to exist. I withdraw into myself to such a degree that I cannot feel the world around me or interact with those present, but I can still hear and see what is transpiring around myself. I cannot speak but I can listen. The experience is perhaps akin to watching a 3D movie. The objects around you are there but they are not really there. They are real yet they are as the wind. A reality all its own that cannot be grasped within your hands. That is kind of how I experience life when I cocoon, and due to Tom's actions and the insecurity they brought on, I shut down once again. However, it wasn't only Tom's part in all this that made me afraid. It was also Betty. After Tom had relocated to his room and before I fully cocooned, I told Betty that I was feeling unwell and unsafe as a result of what had happened. Betty's response to me was "we'll, this is a psych ward." She then returned to the TV room to oversee the rest of the patients and their meals. This comment did not relieve my tension but only added to it. Within a minute I collapsed onto the floor, and within the eyes of the medical staff present I was catatonic once again. This accounted for Betty as well as the chief nurse on duty. They placed me in a chair next to the reception desk and left me there to sit for ten minutes or so. I do not know how long I remained there, but it was such a sufficient amount of time that even I recall its passage. I also remember patients coming up to me to see if I was alright. Most especially Gail. I could tell she was a mother, for Gail had her tender moments and this was one of them. She knew why I was collapsing inward even if the medical staff did not. I had literally been frightened out of my mind.

As a result of my mannequin like state several doctors were eventually called to my aid. My unofficial standby drug which had been given to me when I first entered the ER was again administered, twice. Once by oral tablet, I believe, and when that did not work I was injected via a syringe. My memory of this time is not perfectly clear as I could not interact or feel what was being done to me. What I remember are the words that were being spoken. That word was Ativan. It worked quickly, although to be perfectly clear I felt I was overdosed. I felt as though I were jumping out of my skin. I quickly returned to the real world and began to spit up and speak, one after the other. One of the nurses, who proved most kind, she sat with me for a time and played some music on her phone. Peace, of a sort, had returned to me. Albeit briefly.

As if waiting for another opportunity to torture me, Tom appeared again. As soon as the nurse left my room, Tom entered the scene to utilize my bathroom one last time. Terrified of being alone in my room with this insane person I rolled myself out of bed and crawled through the doorway, forcing it to slam behind me. I then screamed for help while trying to keep Tom in my room with the weight of my body. That tactic failed, for I only weighed 180lbs at the time, and he was easily able to open the door and push me out of the way. Without even looking at me I could see the evil held within his eyes. A face absent a smile yet still a smile was there. Tom walked away in triumph, and as if he were soaking up my fear.

What happened next I do not know. My legs still weren't working but I was wide awake thanks to the Ativan. Even so, I believe I suffered another full blown panic attack. I cannot be certain. The next thing I knew I was in a wheelchair in the TV room with Gail, trying to calm down. She was doing the best she could to get my mind off of recent events when Tom made his entrance into the TV room. It was not enough to torture me and threaten me in the privacy of my own room, Tom seemed to be on a hellbent mission to destroy me and embarrass me publicly and thoroughly. Perhaps his intentions were worse, I will never know. What I can relay is that events which would come to pass, actions between Tom toward hospital staff, these actions have convinced me that during those first hours of Tom's presence in the psych ward I was more than likely in very serious danger. At the current moment in time, one that witnessed Tom, myself and Gail in the TV room together, I was safe if terrified. For we were in full view of the staff behind the reception desk, along with its big glass wall. For my part, all I could do was retreat. I went back to my room when something Heaven sent occurred. One of the staff members suggested having myself locked into my room at night, As in permanently having my door locked, so that only I could open it from the inside, and of course the hospital staff with a key. Of course this meant sleeping in a freezing cold room, but the knowledge that I would be able to sleep soundly more than made up for the cold. I'd had no idea that such a thing was even possible or allowed, and of course I immediately agreed. Seeing as it was time for bed and evening meds were to be distributed shortly, combined with the fact that I'd just received a large dose of Ativan, I was spent and knew I'd be out cold shortly. My door was quickly locked from the outside and I was locked in. I felt secure and fell asleep immediately. It was the sleep of the unfortunate, the depressed and the drugged but I slept until six-thirty the following morning. Nearly ten hours of uninterrupted rest. Upon awakening I left my room, a little gingerly I might add, in order to see what time it was. I looked at the big clock in the office and saw that the TV room would be opening in thirty minutes. Along with that, coffee would be served. Gail's door was still open and she saw me pass on by. My friend came out of her room and talked with me during those minutes before coffee and TV. We spoke of the events of the night prior as well as the insane amount of sleep we were suddenly getting. Gail made me feel better. Not safer mind you, in that I do not believe she could have rescued me should Tom seek me out. It just felt good to have a friend to talk to and not be alone in that long, dark hallway while everyone else was still asleep.

As life often proves to be circular in nature, the time would soon come when our roles would be reversed. It was a time that was approaching, and it had its sights set on Gail. I would be there for her as she was now for me, that's what friends are for. In a place with so little kindness one must cling onto what one has with all ones might. It is the nature of a psych ward that light and warmth can be difficult to find, especially in the early morning hours before the doctor comes to call. The wait for his appearance can be exceedingly long.

Chapter 6.
Tuesday, November 7th, 2023.

After a mercifully uneventful breakfast I was called to my customary morning visit with my psychiatrist. As I recall, this meeting was not held in his his make-shift office just off the reception desk. We met in the much warmer TV room at the opposite end of the hallway. As best as I can remember the broken television was off at this point, and the psychiatrist and I had our daily meeting together in silence. A visit which was always measured in minutes. We discussed my medication, of course, and how much it was improving my nightly rest, as well as my daytime anxiety. We also discussed Tom, and what had been going on with him since his unpleasant arrival. Strange, looking back at these events now. Tom's intrusion into my life seems so much longer and destructive than it really was. I was only around him for a matter of days yet those days seemed much, much longer while events played themselves out. Back to the point, the psychiatrist stated that Tom would not be a problem anymore and that he would talk to the nurses about keeping a closer eye on him. He stated that the rest of my time there would be uneventful. I was of course grateful for his understanding and intervention. Especially since I had no idea how much longer I would be confined to the psych ward. Would it be days, weeks or months? Unbeknownst to me was that the psychiatrist was planning on releasing me in two days. I knew I was doing better but I knew that I was not well enough for discharge. The panic was still there within me, just below the surface and ready to erupt at any time. These were feelings and sensations that I was only just learning to notice and understand, however I could not articulate the fear as of yet. I still suffered from bouts of anxiety throughout the day as well as small panic attacks. I knew that once I was released these things would prove problematic. Yet, that was in the future and I still had no knowledge of my impending departure. I hoped for the best and that there would be time for healing from mental illness and from the memories accumulating in the hospital.

It was a great relief to hear that for whatever reasons I'd not have to worry about Tom anymore. When the psychiatrist said something, it was always the case. As it proved to be with Tom. Tom did not try to enter my room again, as far as I know. Of course it was locked, so he couldn't gain entry. However, he did not make any threatening gestures toward me from that hour on. As a matter of fact, when we were in group therapy that day, throwing the ball around and playing Jeopardy, he was cordial. Tom even smiled at me and apologized to me for his actions. It was quite a shock. Forgiving in nature, I accepted his apology and prayed that what was in the past was now in the realm of what was. In group therapy Tom was as everyone else. He participated, albeit forcibly so, and did not cause a single problem for staff or patient alike. To this day I cannot explain the transformation in him, although I'd guessed it was medically induced. He was drugged. I have no proof of this, but to go from inspiring terror to being friendly in such a short space of time, something had to have happened. It is possible that someone on staff told Tom what ultimately happens to people who chronically misbehave. They are locked in a room with a bed or chair and strapped down tightly so that they cannot move. The only body part which is capable of movement is one arm and only for one hour. After that hour passes, that arm is restrained and the second arm is released. From my point of view, this knowledge is enough to inspire good behavior in just about anyone. Whatever the case, it was not my business to know what was done or said so I did not ask. I simply accepted his absence and tried to focus on my own problems, of which there were many.

Perhaps not chief among my own problems, but definitely weighing heavily on my mind was Gail. She had taken my advice and continued calling her daughter each day. Gail was eventually able to get ahold of her daughter. The first few phone calls were rough on Gail, and she needed a shoulder to cry on. One which I readily offered. During these conversations it was revealed that Gail's daughter refused to let her return to her home. Gail was for all intents and purposes homeless. Several days passed with this knowledge that when Gail was discharged, she'd have nowhere to go. Gail, overall was recovering from what brought her to the psych ward. Being homeless however, seemed to counter any progress on the medical front. Gail was down and depressed all Sunday and Money. However, Tuesday proved to be the breakthrough. Gail was discharged around three in the afternoon, and her daughter came to get her. Gail returned to her daughters home to continue onward with her life, hopefully minus drug use. That, I will never know. I've not heard from Gail since I waved good-bye on that Tuesday in November 2023 and she was gone. I will say this. It is amazing to me how quickly events play out once it is your turn to leave. A patient is told they are being discharged and within a matter of hours they are but a memory. A seat no longer occupied during mealtime.

Time indeed flies, and with it so many feelings and emotions. It was only that very morning that I was dealing with the stress of Tom's abusive behavior and Gail's homelessness, by mid afternoon he had changed and Gail was gone. I barely got to say good-bye to her. After her departure I was alone in the TV room once again just as I'd been the prior Friday. Of course I'd met other people since then. There were quite a number of people in the psych ward at that time. However, some did not want to talk, others didn't leave their rooms all that much, and many had been discharged on Monday. To say there was a revolving door would be an understatement. That door moved swiftly and continuously. Of course I was glad to see the people I'd come to know and like be released to their families. Still, a big part of me missed them greatly. However, one thing remained true, I was still there and in need of support. There was still work for me to do prior to my release. As I've said I had no idea my discharge was being planned. As far as I knew my stay was indefinite, or at least until I could take care of myself again, and so I continued on, doing what I was told to do and giving my best effort at showing some improvement each day.

Some days that meant taking a shower or shaving. Others, changing my clothes or interacting with the other patients a little bit more. Even those small things were seen as huge advances in the psych ward, where some people cannot even do basic body care. There were people there who'd been there for a week and had not showered once. Of course, maybe that has something to do with the showers themselves. Until I was told by other patients how to use them properly I'd never had to endure such a cold shower before! There was no way that I could have known that the hospitals plumbing was so bad that you had to let the warm water run for ten minutes before getting entering the shower stall. If you didn't do that, showers were brief and quick, because they were just as cold as the rooms we slept in. I'll also record this for posterity. The psych ward's showers were showers in name and presentation only. The water was cold and it ran in a trickle. It was possible to get oneself clean with the all in one body-hair wash we were given, however the water ran so slowly that a five minute shower would easily take ten. Ten minutes in that cold water felt like an eternity. It wasn't until Gail told me to let the water run that I was able to take a comfortably warm shower. The showers, as cold as they could be were not a serious problem nor concern, just an annoyance. What was troubling was the loneliness I felt. Fortunately that proved to be short lived. My mother and my friend Kimberly had visited me on Sunday. A visit which h ad brought great relief to my mind. However, once they were gone I felt lonelier than before they came. I missed my life. Now, with Gail gone, the silence was truly setting in to my soul.

It seems that in my quest for improved mental capabilities I was not meant to be completely alone. For just as Gail left my life forever, enter a woman I shall refer to as Heather. About fifty-five and five foot five, she had blondish-grey hair and she was married. Someone had brought her a pair of footsie-pajama's from home and she wore those during her stay. Hers was a cute outfit! Simply adorable.

Heather proved to be a lot like Gail. Friendly, talkative and needing someone to interact with. She needed a friend. She chose me for that role. I remember sitting in the TV room playing solitaire, for by this time several decks of cards had been donated to the unit. In walks Heather, and she sits down next to me and asks me if she were invading my space. I said of course not, I was glad to meet her. We talked for as long as time allowed, for by this time the students were soon to return and it would officially be group time again. We had to participate. I think we played games of Bingo that day, but I could be mistaken. It was tiring having to talk to all of those students as well play a game I wasn't truly in the mood to play. It's not just the forced socialization, but when you're put on a new sedative, and you're being given pills all day long, pills that make you sleepy, one of the last things you want to do is play Bingo. It's hard enough to pay attention to the television set without nodding off. Social interaction became incredibly difficult. Of course it was done, but not without drawing on reserves that I did not know I'd had.

Time, fortunately passed us by quickly. The students were gone and dinner was quickly wheeled in. Exhausted, I inhaled mine and shortly thereafter returned to my room to brush my teeth and lay down. My rest was brief. A matter of minutes, if that. In so short a time I was quickly disturbed by a commotion coming from the TV room. Little did I know that what had affected me so intimately was now on display for all to see.

I hurried back to see what was going on and not much to my surprise, it was Tom. He had verbally assaulted the staff member who was serving dinner, and that would be Betty. A no-nonsense, military minded style individual who nobody dare cross. Only Tom had. He also came close to physically assaulting Betty as well. The reason, as I came to learn of it, was that Tom did not order a dinner for himself and therefore did not receive one. When this fact had been discovered Tom had been verbally asked what he wanted for dinner and he uttered no response. Therefore, he had received no meal with the rest of us. Betty was quick in ordering a supper for Tom, however something set him off and he became violent. A verbal barrage launched at Betty, and a near attack on her person. Instead, one of the chairs became the target of his fury. By the time I had arrived the two were in a stare-down, Betty was the obvious victor. The TV room quickly cleared out, Heather and I retreated down the hall to the warmer TV room. This is where Heather told me about the events that had commenced after I'd finished dinner and left.

I did not see much of Tom after that incident. There was one instance where I heard one of the psychiatrists talking to Tom later that night. The next day, the social worker had him seated in the TV room, and was in deep discussion with Tom about what would happen upon his discharge, or if he could get discharged. His discharge wasn't assured anytime soon. Other than these two occasions, I did not see Tom again. I don't want to speculate about where he was, but he was not around the rest of us, which made my time in the psych ward all the better.

The time was now around 7:00pm and I would be remiss if I did not relate details about another new arrival to the psych ward. Having arrived about twenty-four hours previously, she was an eye opener for me. A confirmation of what my grandmother had told me about institutions like this forty-years prior. For my grandmother had worked in a psych ward and, for a period of time was a patient in that same unit. She would often tell me stories about what went on in psychiatric institutions. I never knew if they were true or not. Toward the end of my stay in the psych ward I was to learn that her tales were indeed true, for what she told me was demonstrated by this new arrival. Confined to a wheel-chair and unable to walk or communicate was a young woman, about twenty-five or so, and she was an empty vessel. Something Gail had the unfortunate pleasure of waking up to on the last day of her stay.

Sleeping with her door open as she always did, Gail was asleep in bed when she heard a noise. Gail turned around and saw this woman, whom I will refer to as Natasha, sitting at the side of her bed, staring at her from her wheel chair. The effect of someone being in your room, male or female, when they have no right to be there is scary for anyone. When it happened to Gail it freaked her out majorly. She screamed and hollered to high Heaven, waking up the entire ward. Natasha, seemingly not knowing the difference between right and wrong was more or less infantile in her thinking. She thought she had to use the bathroom and did not know where it was, even though there was one in her room. She sought Gail out for assistance. It was an intrusion that was not received well and hospital staff quickly intervened in the verbal tongue lashing Gail was in the process of giving Natasha. This intervention did not help matters in the long run, because Natasha could not understand that what she was doing was scaring the other patients. She continued to enter their rooms and provoke fear in each person she sought help from. The fact that she also sought sexual favors from others in the unit, from both doctors and patients, only made everyone all the more leery of her. Add this. For whatever reason Natasha was only given a hospital gown to wear and nothing underneath it. Nothing more whatsoever. A fact that was impossible to ignore when she would wheel herself down the hallway, her gown in a position which left little to the imagination. She had no conception of modesty whatsoever, and seemed completely unaware that her gown was open, or that she was even wearing clothes at all. There was something about this woman that was almost scary. Not that she would or could hurt anyone, but in that her mental troubles made it impossible to know what she would do or say next. Of all the people I met during my time in the psych ward, Natasha was indeed the most troubled. Physically, emotionally, mentally, perhaps even spiritually, anything and everything that made Natasha a person, it all was gone. When I'd see her I would see an adult woman who could not eat or use the rest room on her own. At least, not safely. Natasha was a woman with major issues. Some of which went beyond anything this world could rationally explain.

My last memory of Natasha is the eeriest. On my last night spent in the psych ward, there were voices and music coming out of Natasha's room. Only they were not her voice, nor did the voices belong to any of the other patients in the unit. Of course I do not know all the doctors in the hospital, and it could have been them. Only doctors don't speak that loudly to patients in casual conversation. It just didn't seem feasible that the voices heard coming from Natasha's room were coming from her. Nor did it seem likely that they were coming from anyone else who could possibly be in with her. Where the voices came from and who did they belonged to is a question I will never know the answer to, for I just turned myself over and went back to sleep. All the while trying to shut out the strange music drifting down the halls. For the song that was being sung was Take Me Out to the Ballgame. Only nobody was around who could have been singing it.

Chapter 7.
Wednesday, November 8th, 2023 through
Friday, November 10th, 2023

Wednesday, November 8th, 2023 was the one week anniversary of my crash, or so it seemed at the time. Looking back over the course of events leading up to the evening of November 1st, and continuing into the morning of November 2nd, I can now see that the seeds of my mental illness were planted much further back than that first of November. The roots stretch as far back in time as the previous August, and quite possibly even further into the past. August however was key. From August until October 2023 I'd suffered a great deal of ill health. It seemed that just as one malady was taken care of another would follow. During those three months I did not have one day of good health, and was on a merry-go-round of medications, some of which resulted in side effects that were worse than the illness. This was a period of personal purgatory, spent almost entirely on my sofa and in my bed. Always with the hope that next week would be the week I'd be well and on my feet again. Only, that hoped for destination never came into view. I got worse until the day of my mental collapse, when I could physically and mentally take no more.

    As mentioned prior, due to gastro-intestinal issues I'd suffered an anal tear and this caused me no end of suffering. The gastroenterologist I went to see on November 1st prescribed some cream for the pain and healing, and I must say that the cream did help a great deal. However, due to the physical anguish I was enduring and the pain being a panic trigger, my mental state had deteriorated drastically. Pain in general was and still is a huge problem for me, as well as for my anxiety and panic attacks. Back in October 2023, when the anal tear first occurred, I could not handle that level of pain along with the stress of the other health issues I'd been having. Pain, panic and stress, combine these with the loss of several of my kitties, my best friends, well, it was all too much for my mind to handle. As has been covered in this book, my mind cracked and I fell into a ravine. Fortunately, even with the past working against me, after one weeks treatment in the psych ward I was on the mend. I was at the beginning of what turned out to be a long journey. One of healing and good mental health. As I would later be told, there were no quick fixes for a mental breakdown. Only through the help of my own psychiatrist and therapist, neither which I had yet, would I be able to overcome the obstacles which lay before me. One of which was quickly thrust upon me.

    After the dramatic events of the day prior, Wednesday started off in as calm a manner as can be. Gail was gone, Heather had arrived. Tom was nowhere to be seen. As

I awakened I still had not been told that my discharge was set for the next day. As far as I was aware, I was in the psych ward until I'd recovered and been restored to whatever normal might be. This being my first time in the psych ward I simply did not know how things like that worked. In ignorance, I lived each day as it came, not knowing nor really caring when I'd be released.

Wednesday itself was as any other day had been, and it consisted mostly of an extremely long schedule of group activities in addition to arts and crafts. One group right after another without any real letup. It was like being in high school again. Going from class to class and listening to someone talk for an hour. During what few off-hours we were allotted I would sit and talk with Heather about her life, or try desperately to stay out of Natasha's way. For someone who could not speak a coherent sentence this young lady had a way of being the center of attention time after time.

One unfortunate instance in particular comes to mind. One in where Natasha was given some coffee to drink. In a psych ward nothing is as it seems. Natasha did not drink coffee, she ate it, along with some packets of sugar substitute she procured from the coffee cart. Upon receiving her drink, Natasha went about methodically emptying the packets onto the table situated directly in front of her. She then stuffed the paper packets into her coffee. What a mess, to say the least. The paper that now lay crammed into her styrofoam cup had absorbed most of if not all of her coffee. There were no staff on duty in the TV room and so Natasha was left to her own devices. This was most certainly not good for someone in her delicate mental state. Another of the patients eventually tried to assist the young woman and get her a fresh cup of coffee only to be rebuffered in ferocious fashion akin to a lioness protecting her cubs. Natasha did not want help nor guidance. Unfortunately, she was to be left alone to eat her creation. That, as they say, was that. It's what she wanted. With no staff around to tell her no, she consumed what she had made, to the horror of all onlookers. Most especially Heather and myself.

My memory fails me in the immediately aftermath of Natasha's drink. I believe I went to take a nap, skipping the group that was planned for that hour. I was physically drained after the morning activities. Afterward, my activities consisted of looking out of the large windows of my favorite TV room for quite a long spell. Nobody else was about because they were in group, so I had the TV room and the window all to myself. This window afforded me a view of the comings and goings of people into and out of the hospital on a rainy November afternoon. I remember feeling envious of the raindrops falling on the ground. They were free, whereas I was behind locked door. I told myself that one day I'd be free and healthy again. Not today but one day. Until then, I had my friend the television, the window, the puzzles and the playing cards. When I was alone in the TV room I would often reflect on the past. In particular all of my past outings that took me past this very building and this very window. My ignorance of this place during all those drive-bys seemed surreal somehow. For I never knew that I was driving by the window of a psych ward. One which I would occupy one dark and drizzly day. This day, I watched the cars of many drive passed, their occupants oblivious of the fact that they were now passing a psych ward. I wondered, would one of those drivers or passengers be in my spot one day? Thinking the thoughts I am think? There were no hospital signs outside the building I was in, and the windows were tinted black. Nobody could see in. I would sit and watch, so incredibly envious of the people who were mentally fit and that's how the one week anniversary of my fall proceeded. Sitting, watching, wondering and contemplating life. Sometimes I'd interact with the other patients, mostly Heather. If my memory is correct a lot of people left this day. Some discharged, others not. They were either being moved on to other facilities or going home. The psych ward had a strange, quiet emptiness about it on Wednesday night. As I recall I was the only one there who wanted a shower and had my pick of either shower room, and I was the only one in it. This proved to be the quiet before the storm. Thursday proved to be far more dramatic.

As I've mentioned several times, Thursday was my scheduled date of discharge, which I discovered Thursday morning as I spoke with my psychiatrist. However, I was not ready to leave. Not by a long shot. I wanted to leave, of course. I wanted to go home and be with my kitties more than anything in the world. Leaving was all anyone really talked about with any regularity. We'd dream of our discharge day, what we'd do when we got out and how we'd never come back to this place again. Because, truth be told, it wasn't our fault that we were in the psych ward to begin with. The reason was almost always the same too. It was always someone else's fault that a patient had been committed. From what I could gather from staff, the most often asked question was "when am I going home?" I even heard one nurse say "the more you ask when you're going home, the longer you're going to be here." It's been over a year and I still don't fully understand that response. I personally never inquired about my day of discharge. It's not that I didn't want to leave, I just knew that I was still scared out of my mind, and I was only at the beginning of the long path toward recovery. I knew I was where I belonged. I figured I wasn't getting out for a while so why bother asking? The news that I was to be discharged that day came to me as quite a shock. I simply was not ready to leave, which I told the psychiatrist. He gave me a short lecture about how this unit was only temporary and that I couldn't stay there forever, but he understood my position. I felt safe in the psych ward. There were doctors, nurses and staff to see that nothing bad happened to me. The incidents with Tom being set aside, he was correct, I was protected and I was safe. The psychiatrist agreed to keep me one more day and see how I felt the following morning. All things being as they were, that was perfectly fine with me. I was eating more than I'd eaten in months, sleeping more than I'd slept in I can't say how long, and I was actually around people for a change. Every day, at that. Sure, it was a psych ward, but it did offer protection from the outside world and all the responsibilities that go along with being in it. For someone who had just come from a situation where he could not even walk and was suffering non-stop panic attacks, the psych ward, with its many problems was not the worst place in the world to be. It wasn't the best, but it certainly wasn't the worst. I still reserve the worst spot in the world as being the ER downstairs, which was the prelude to my commitment. That place is Hell on Earth.

Had life continued on as it was at that moment, I do not know that I'd have been released the following day, as eventually occurred. It was what transpired next that sent me back into a state of near constant anxiety, borderline by panic attacks and on my way out of the psych ward.

It was late Thursday morning and I was endeavoring to make something or other during arts and crafts. I honestly don't remember much, such was the shock of what was to come. What I do remember is that music was playing and everything seemed fine, when all of a sudden two women entered the art room. I'd never seen them before. They called my name. I quickly followed them out into the hallway where they told me the reason for their visit. They worked with the city courts, and they handed me some paperwork, none of which did I understand. What the women told me was that since I'd been forcibly committed on my intake, I had to have a court hearing regarding my placement into the psych ward. My court appointed attorney would be getting in touch with me that afternoon via telephone, and that as they say, is that. The women left me standing there, completely befuddled and in shock. I went back into the art room with my paper in hand not knowing what had just happened. Thankfully, the person who ran the arts and crafts program had been involved with the psych ward for many, many years and she advised me on what had just occurred, and what to do next.

More than likely, since I was in no proper state of mind to make decisions for myself when I entered the ER, the doctor signed my commitment papers. The fact that I had agreed to go to the psych ward voluntarily was irrelevant. My consent only cleared the way to have me sent up when they were ready to receive me. Legally, my agreeing to go into the psych ward had no bearing on my personal legal status as a patient. Because of this, a hearing had to be held regarding my commitment. I could fight it, which would lengthen my stay in the psych ward, possibly by several days, or I could decline the hearing, sign some papers and my case would not go before a judge. It was suggested by this kind woman that my best interest was to sign the paper and not fight my commitment, instantaneously clearing the way for my release. Since I was due to be discharged on Friday, the very next day, there was not much of a decision to be made.

Therefore, I spoke with my court appointed attorney, signed the papers and I was free to leave when my psychiatrist discharged me the following morning.

I say this most emphatically. Upon receiving the paperwork and knowledge of my involvement with the court system, and the legal complexity of the paperwork as well as my unstable state of mind, I was overcome with anxiety and fear and not making the best decisions for myself or my future. When a person like me suffers anxiety they do what they must to relieve themselves of the fear of the moment, or the triggering event. I wanted to get away from the lawyers and judges and anyone who could feasibly keep me trapped in this place against my will, even to my own detriment. I was now completely, one-hundred percent ready to go home, even though I knew that I wasn't mentally ready to leave and my medication wasn't fully covering me. The future didn't matter to me. I wanted the fear gone. It doesn't matter that all these months later I know there was nothing to be afraid of and everything was exactly as it was told to me, at the time these events took place I would not listen. I could not listen. As a result, on Friday morning at 10:30am I was officially released from the hospital. My mother came to drive me home. There, a friend waited for me. She was to take care of me during those first two months I was out of the hospital. I will admit, I needed a lot of care. A babysitter, a cook, a maid, and a friend. I was still unable to look after myself as I had when I was mentally fit.

These events only go on to prove that psychiatric patients shouldn't be consulted as to when they want to leave the psych ward. I suffered those first few days after my discharge. I did not have my own psychiatrist nor my own therapist yet, both of which were desperately needed. I had my medication, but it wasn't fully doing the job. I was having breakthrough panic attacks and episodes of cocooning, a.k.a. catatonia. The shock and strain of being home again, the place where everything had so recently happened, combined with inadequate medication was simply too much for me. So much so that only two days later, on Sunday, November 12th, I was back in the hospital once again. It was Sunday night around 6:00pm which saw me being wheeled by ambulance back into the very same ER I'd been in just over a week prior. Not only the same ER but I was now in the very same spot underneath that horrid light that had shone in my face all day and night. To make matters worse, the same nurse was on duty. Adam. I was once again officially entered into their records as a catatonic upon entry. I could not move nor speak. I'd come full circle. I knew it and I couldn't handle that fact. I was not going back to the psych ward, anymore than I was going to stay in this nightmare of an emergency room one second longer than I had to. I was going home, my mental condition be damned.

Remembering me from my previous stay, Adam quickly transferred me to an isolation room found at the back of the ER. I was not about to let myself sit in that little cubby hole for eighteen hours, and so I told the doctor on duty that I was only recently from the psych ward two days prior, and was having problems with anxiety. Which was true, just not the full scope of the truth. I was going to start seeing a new psychiatrist shortly, as well as a therapist, but I needed something to cover the stretches where the medication I was on was not working. The doctor prescribed something for me and discharged me faster than I ever had been before. Evidentially this doctor, a person who had not been present upon my earlier stay had heard of my antics and was relieved to not have me as a problem patient. Reversely, I was never so grateful to leave any place in my life. I swore to myself that I'd never, ever go back there again. I wouldn't listen to anyone who told me that I needed to go back to that ER for any reason. It's a promise I've kept. Certainly, I've been back to a hospital in the last year and a half, as well as to an emergency room. Just not that particular hospital nor that particular ER. Where I go now is much calmer and has doctors and nurses whom actually demonstrate care for all patients. Even so, I still suffer greatly because of my time spent in that first emergency room. The memories and emotions are still as raw as when they were first formed. Let me leave you with this bitter taste from my own mouth. There are places in this world that are not good places to be. That emergency room is most certainly one of them.

    The first few months following my release back into the world were strange and they were difficult. On the one had, everything was familiar. The same home, the same pets, the same friends. On the other hand, everyone and everything seemed different. It was as if I were behind a darkened glass looking at what was once everyday life, only now all was shaded in shadow. It was only with the help of my friend who was caring for me, as well as a good psychiatrist that I started to improve. My new psychiatrist has always been there for me, even when needed at inconvenient times. There were certainly plenty of those during the beginning. The first therapist I found, unfortunately, was not very helpful. His idea of helping a patient was getting them back into the world and interacting with people. Whereas my psychiatrist was trying to find a medication that didn't make me want to sleep sixteen hours a day. Their treatment plans didn't merge very well at all. I could not do what the therapist wanted and eventually he ghosted me. One week here, the next gone. Not just from my life but from the company he worked for. Thus, I was left with the task of finding a new therapist, once again. Fortunately someone with my insurance company knew a therapist and this new therapist has been absolutely fantastic. Everything the first therapist hadn't been, she is. I think she is one of the smartest people I've ever met.

    Even with the help of a psychiatrist and therapist I still struggle with social anxiety as well as getting out of the house, only not quite as much as I used to. When I first left the hospital I was scared to death to be in a public place because I did not know what to say or how to act. I'd completely forgotten how to act in public and this terrified me. That aspect of my mental illness has lessened considerably over time. With medication and therapy. I've remembered how to be sociable.

    The time of my hospitalization, November 2nd through November 10th, 2023 will forever be with me. All of it. The good and the bad. These memories cross a spectrum as vast as my minds eye can see. However, I know this was an event that had to have happened. There was simply no way that I could have endured any longer on my own. I needed help and I was fortunate to receive it. I can wish all I want that everything had gone perfectly. That all the nurses were professional and that all the patients were meek and mild, but we do not live in a perfect world. Our worlds imperfections are why people end up in the psych ward in the first place. Sometimes we can't cope with the negativity in our lives, and that stress is too much to take. When that happens we need help, and the first person to admit this need must be us. People can tell one another time and again that they need to be helped, but until we admit it to ourselves nothing can change in our lives. Nothing will improve. Once we finally accept the offered help things do change for the better. Perhaps not as quickly as we'd like, but things will change for the better, over time. We just need patience, along the help of those who care about us.

Epilogue.
Monday, February 17th, 2025.

It has been fifteen months since the last ambulance ride which delivered me into the hands of the ER. An enormous amount of time has passed, to be sure. Considering where I came from, one day can be and often is an eternity. In the beginning, those first few days after my discharge, I checked off each day that I was safely in my home, in front of the TV with my cats, safe and secure. Each setting sun witnessed in freedom counted as a victory to be proud of. Time accumulated and shortly I started counting off the weeks. As the weeks accumulated, months would be noted as having gone by. In all this time I've never once returned to that horrid emergency room nor the psych ward.

When I was a patient I never thought so much time could or would pass uneventfully. That is, without being carted off via ambulance to the hospital several times a month. Having gone through those motions, being carted away seven times in thirty or so days, it certainly seemed like any resemblance of mental health was far away. However, time progressed and I was given the correct medication for my condition, as well as something my metabolism could properly digest within a certain time period. The stray thoughts went away, the fire of fear dwindled and I began to understand that I did not need the crutch of on-call medical help. This was a slow discovery and one that I didn't even know was dawning while it was occurring. Months simply passed me by and the medication began to do its job. A stable, mostly normal daily life ensued. Of course, like a lot of people with anxiety disorders I still suffer. I am not by any means cured. I still deal with sudden bursts of anxiety that seemingly come out of nowhere and without provocation, but nothing like the cocooning stage that I suffered during October and November 2023. Within the last year that particular event has only occurred once. My overall anxiety has lessened greatly.

Of course what works for one person won't necessarily work for another. One persons time frame won't apply to others. Everyone is unique and has their own set of circumstances to deal with. However, from first hand experience I've noted the effect of what proper medical help can do to calm panic, fear, terror, depression and anxiety. These things can be relieved if not resolved. A somewhat normal life can be lived. Joy can be restored and return to day to day living. By no means is it an easy path, nor is it one that is quickly traveled. It's very bumpy and there are forks in the road that will lead to dead ends. However, if you keep trying to make an ascent, if you choose to continue with the journey you will eventually end up in a good place. From my own experience, not being able to get up off of my hallway floor and walk to the present day, I've published seven books in a little over a year. When just a little over a year ago I didn't know if I'd ever write again. Mental illness isn't the end of the road, it's a part of the road that's difficult to traverse. Some of its obstacles can be conquered, while others may be walked around. Patience is a must, even though at times it is difficult to demonstrate. Patience is and always will be needed every day one struggles with mental illness. If you persevere, days will turn into years, with some days better than others, but overall improvement in thought and feeling can be achieved.

Of course, because of what has happened and the medication I am on, I feel that I will never again be the person I was before my mental collapse. Be that as it may, I've come to realize that the person I am becoming is not such a bad fellow, either. I still have what's important to me. My cats are still with me, I have my constant stream of television all morning and afternoon, and of course my writing. Not to mention the basics of life. Food and drink in my fridge as well as a roof over my head. Then there are the doctors who help me make it through each day with all my medications. I could not make it without their wisdom, teachings and advice, and of course the medication.

To be honest, there are a lot of pills I have to take each day. However, they are needed. I know that my current stability is based on the continued taking of what I've been prescribed. I might feel fine some days, but I'm not. The medication is what is making me feel better. Like an army, my medication fights the root causes of anxiety. The traumatic memories of my long past combined with recollections of more recent events. Without the doctors and the medication I am on I know that I would be right back where I was on November 2nd, 2023. Back on my way to some psych ward because I cannot endure without the help I now have. In order to maintain stability one needs a strong foundation. With mental illness, that foundation is doing what you're supposed to do. What you've been told by those you've trusted to treat you.

In addition to all that's been described above, there is also my emotional support cat, Dr. Chip. He whom I've had since he was a few weeks old. He is almost always by my side and always here when I need him most. I don't know how he knows, but he knows when I'm about to have an anxiety attack. He'll come up to me, jump on my stomach and headbutt me in the face. Then stay by me while we ride through it together. Afterwards, he runs off to the bathroom to sit on the toilet. Why? I don't know. It's just Dr. Chip being Dr. Chip!

As for the long term effects of having been in the psych ward, of course they are there. The memories of having my freedom taken from me, of the loneliness experienced alone in my room at night, the fear experienced and the longing for home. However, I realize that most of my time there was what it was supposed to be. Long and lonely and reflective. A time to mentally recuperate, if you will. Of course the rooms and showers could have been warmer, and the patients monitored more carefully. Even so, it was what it was. It was a psych ward. My real psychological scars come from my time spent in the emergency room. The hours I spent in a ongoing state of extreme panic with no help coming. These are the memories that truly haunt my dreams. These are the images of what nightmares are made from. The memory of being helpless and feeling hopeless, without a soul around offering any amount of comfort. Of course, these are just memories and overall cannot physically hurt me. Even so, the lingering anxiety over what I felt in that emergency room is with me still.

I always thought that hospitals were supposed to be a place of healing. That was until November 2nd, 2023. It was then that I was given a first class ticket to purgatory. On that day I fully realized that hospitals can make things both mentally and physically worse. More, they can destroy a person emotionally. When staff are hired who prove over time that they will continually neglect their patients, that is wrong. I wasn't the only patient left to suffer throughout that day and into the night. There were screams of others in torment. This place was as close to a hell as I'd ever come on Earth, and it's not an experience I would ever wish on my worst enemy. Some things should not be allowed to occur. Some places should not be allowed to exist, yet unfortunately they are and do. The world is considerably worse off because of man made purgatories like the emergency room I was in, and those who partake in its sins.

Should you or someone you know, through no fault of their own fall into a dark ravine of life, know that it's not the end. A fall can be fast and go very deep, and it's so easy to let the gravity of the moment take one and do with one what it will. Then, when the end is reached and one comes to rest they look up and see how far they've come, it may seem that climbing out of that ravine and resuming one's place in life is all but impossible. Depending on how deep the fall was and how injured one is, it could take years to make one's way into the light again. If a person keeps on moving and keeps on climbing they'll eventually make it out and be back onto the path that God has set before them. What's important to remember is that one never give up trying to achieve victory, in whatever fashion victory may come in. Never let you or anyone around you become accustomed or comfortable with being in a dark ravine when there is so much else in life to see, and so very much to accomplish and enjoy. For when one eventually resurfaces they will be far different than when they fell, and far more capable of appreciating those around who make like worth living. Because, when it comes right down to it, our friends and family will be needed more than ever before. It's these relationships that will keep us going when light once again enters our eyes. Most importantly, keep smiling. For your own simple smile will give you and others the encouragement and protection needed to meet each day that lay ahead. Let your smile be your shield for it will protect you.

Printed in Great Britain
by Amazon